SUMMARY
&ANALYSIS

OF

Educated

A MEMOIR

A GUIDE TO THE BOOK
BY TARA WESTOVER

BY **ZIP**READS

NOTE: This book is a summary and analysis and is meant as a companion to, not a replacement for, the original book.

Please follow this link to purchase a copy of the original book: https://amzn.to/2Cp3ple

TABLE OF CONTENTS

SYNOPSIS.. 6

KEY PLAYERS.. 6

PART I.. 9

CHAPTER 1: Choose the Good 9

CHAPTER 2: The Midwife 10

CHAPTER 3: Cream Shoes...................................... 10

CHAPTER 4: Apache Women 11

CHAPTER 5: Honest Dirt... 12

CHAPTER 6: Shield and Buckler 12

CHAPTER 7: The Lord Will Provide......................... 14

CHAPTER 8: Tiny Harlots 15

CHAPTER 9: Perfect in His generations.................. 15

CHAPTER 10: Shield of Feathers 16

CHAPTER 11: Instinct... 17

CHAPTER 12: Fish Eyes 18

CHAPTER 13: Silence in the Churches.................... 19

CHAPTER 14: My Feet No Longer Touch Earth........ 20

CHAPTER 15: No More a Child 21

CHAPTER 16: Disloyal Man, Disobedient Heaven..... 22

PART II 24

CHAPTER 17: To Keep It Holy 24

CHAPTER 18: Blood and Feathers 24

CHAPTER 19: In the Beginning 25

CHAPTER 20: Recitals of the Fathers 26

CHAPTER 21: Skullcap 26

CHAPTER 22: What We Whispered and What We
Screamed 27

CHAPTER 23: I'm from Idaho 28

CHAPTER 24: A Knight, Errant 29

CHAPTER 25: The Work of Sulphur 29

CHAPTER 26: Waiting for Moving Water 30

CHAPTER 27: If I Were a Woman 30

CHAPTER 28: Pygmalion 31

CHAPTER 29: Graduation 32

PART III 33

CHAPTER 30: Hand of the Almighty 33

CHAPTER 31: Tragedy Then Farce 34

CHAPTER 32: A Brawling Woman in a Wide House .. 34

CHAPTER 33: Sorcery of Physics 35

CHAPTER 34: The Substance of Things 35

CHAPTER 35: West of the Sun..............................36

CHAPTER 36: Four Long Arms, Whirling 37

CHAPTER 37: Gambling for Redemption.................37

CHAPTER 38: Family..38

CHAPTER 39: Watching the Buffalo 38

CHAPTER 40: Educated.......................................39

KEY THEMES.. **41**

The Transformative Power of Education 41

The Deep Hold of Patriarchy 41

The Constant Presence of Religion 42

The Existence of Two Americas 42

EDITORIAL REVIEW **43**

BACKGROUND ON AUTHOR............................. **46**

END OF BOOK SUMMARY...........................**47**

KEY PLAYERS

Tara Westover – the author; youngest of seven siblings

Dad (Gene) – Tara's overbearing, extremely religious father

Mother (Faye) – Tara's mother; a self-taught herbalist and occasional midwife

Tony – Tara's eldest brother

Shawn – Tara's second eldest brother, whose relationship with Tara plays a major role in her eventual estrangement from the family

Tyler – Tara's third eldest brother and the first one to go to college

Luke – Tara's fourth eldest brother

Audrey – Tara's sister, who married early and stayed near their parents' farm with her husband

Richard – Tara's youngest brother, who also went to college after Tara

Grandma-over-in-town – Tara's mother's mother, who hadn't been happy with her daughter's decision to marry Gene

Grandma-down-the-hill – Tara's father's mother, who lived close to the family and shared a love-hate relationship with his son

Charles – Tara's first "normal" friend, whom she met during her play rehearsals in town

Nick – Tara's first boyfriend in college

Drew – Tara's second boyfriend in college

Dr. Kerry – Tara's Jewish history professor at BYU who encouraged her to try for the Cambridge program

Professor Steinberg – Tara's supervisor at King's College, Cambridge, who helped her get the Gates Cambridge Scholarship

SYNOPSIS

Educated is a memoir written by Tara Westover in her early thirties. She was the youngest of seven children, born in 1986 to a Mormon couple living on an isolated farm near a mountain called Buck's Peak in Idaho.

Partly because of religious norms, partly because of his own paranoia, her father forbade formal education and modern medicine, among other things. The children were meant to help their father sell scrap metal from his junkyard or in the occasional construction contracts he managed to get ahold of. Their mother's work as a midwife and traditional medicine woman helped bring in some much-needed extra income, with the latter skill even turning the family relatively prosperous by the time Westover reached her mid-twenties.

Westover, who had remained mostly uneducated till she managed to join Brigham Young University at seventeen, survived this difficult childhood and parental resistance to achieve great academic success, including stints at Harvard and Cambridge.

However, in the process, most of her family, including her parents, ended up disowning her for going against convention and raising her voice against the physical abuse by one of her brothers. Her parents had not resumed talking to her by the time the memoir was published.

PART I

CHAPTER 1: CHOOSE THE GOOD

Westover begins with the strongest memory from her childhood—an imagined memory formed after a story told by her father. It involves gunfights, shouts; her family is huddled in their house, hiding from the Feds. A shot is fired; her mother falls, with a baby in her arms. The baby doesn't make sense as she is the youngest of the seven children.

The rest of the chapter introduces Westover's father and Grandma-down-the-hill. Dad's family had lived at the base of Buck's Peak, Idaho for half a century. Most of his family had moved away, but he stayed, living some distance from his mother and making money from a junkyard and some odd jobs. Dad wasn't a tall man but was able to command a room. Grandma was a force of nature, aggressive and self-possessed.

Grandma and Dad had a bit of a love-hate relationship. She wanted Tara and her siblings to be in school; he considered public school a Government ploy to take children away from God.

Grandma and Grandpa used to spend their winters in Arizona, and one year they offered to take Tara (around seven at the time) along and get her admitted into a school. Tara was tempted, but couldn't gather the courage to disobey her father.

Her thoughts also kept going back to the story referred to at the chapter's beginning: Randy Weaver had lost his wife and son in the notorious Ruby Ridge standoff in Idaho in 1992. Scared that the Feds would come next for their family, Dad began piling up food and collecting guns. She never got to know the end of the story, but it left a strong impression on her.

CHAPTER 2: THE MIDWIFE

To fulfill Dad's plans to go completely off the grid and to complement the measly income from scrapping, Mother had to become a midwife against her wishes. Midwifing changed her as she was in charge of something for the first time in her life. She had already been an herbalist of repute, but midwifing earned her wider respect and got the family some much-needed money.

The chapter also relates a funny incident where, after almost nine years of being born, Tara finally gets a birth certificate. No one in the family seemed to be sure when the children had been born.

CHAPTER 3: CREAM SHOES

Tara's mother, Faye, was born in a respectable family to a seamstress, LaRue (Grandma-over-in-town), and a mailman. LaRue's father had been poor and alcoholic; the social contempt from the Mormon community they lived in made her build a veneer of respectability around her own family. Faye had nice dresses, a life of normalcy, but she rebelled and married the physically impressive and independent-minded Gene against her mother's wishes. Tara, in turn, envied the life her mother had had, worrying about things like the color of her shoes.

Tara knew little about Gene's childhood. Living with a very strict father, he developed fierce opinions about women, the way they should dress, where they should work.

Looking at the one surviving photo from their wedding, Tara finds it difficult to reconcile the untroubled young man with the anxious man she knew to be her father. She couldn't always understand his actions until she came upon the term "bipolar disorder" fourteen years later in college.

p·30 How the paranoia ... carving up his life

CHAPTER 4: APACHE WOMEN

One winter, the family took a road trip to sunny Arizona to visit Grandma-over-in-town because Dad had been in a post-Christmas funk in cold Idaho. During his gradual recovery, he realized that Grandma relied on modern medicine and began berating her every day for being faithless, an agent of the Illuminati.

One day, he suddenly decided the family would drive back home. Tyler, then seventeen, had been driving the car through the night in bad weather. Around six in the morning, he dozed off; the car fell into a ditch, and some of them were injured. The most seriously hurt was Mother, who suffered swellings in the head and experienced forgetfulness and migraines for a very long time.

The chapter title refers to the tribal women whose lives are decided for them even before they are born.

CHAPTER 5: HONEST DIRT

A month after the car accident, Tyler declared he was going to college. Dad was strictly against formal education, but Tyler stood his ground. Dad was also worried that after Tony moving out to drive rigs and Shawn taking off after a quarrel, if Tyler also moved away, he would be left with no crew to build barns.

Tyler had always been different from the other children, orderly and a lover of books and music. Tara felt calm listening to choir music in his company. He had picked up a fair bit of education despite Mother's homeschooling being very sporadic and Dad insisting on hauling all the children for work early in the morning. Once Tyler left for college in August, he rarely came home again.

Sometime later, Tara was surprised to be admonished by Grandma-over-in-town for not washing her hands with soap after using the toilet.

CHAPTER 6: SHIELD AND BUCKLER

Audrey turned fifteen that winter, took two jobs, got a car, and was rarely seen around the house. Luke, sixteen, became the eldest son, and Richard and Tara the grunts in the junkyard. Tara went through a harrowing training period as Dad would chuck pieces of scrap metal into the bin from wherever he was standing, often hitting or just missing her. Dad's response was: "God and angels are here, working right alongside us. They won't let you be hurt" (Kindle Locations 1019-1020).

As her midwife work had taken a hit after the accident, Mother began mixing oils to treat illnesses. She took up something called "muscle testing," which involved asking the body what it needed. She also began doing "energy work," much to Tara's skepticism.

Tyler's leaving for college aroused curiosity in Tara for the first time. She began reading Mormon treatises, the only books in the house, which constituted her first education. Meanwhile, Richard would also spend all his free time reading, even though Dad tried his best to keep both of them busy.

There was an incident in the junkyard where Tara almost got buried under a pile of scrap. Unsure if Dad would bother to ensure she was safe before dumping the scrap over her, she used her own presence of mind to come away with just a gash in the knee. This accident seemed to spark the first sign of rebellion in her—she expressed her desire to go to school but was convinced by Dad that she was at fault for wanting it.

CHAPTER 7: THE LORD WILL PROVIDE

One day the following summer, Tara was at home working on Mother's Rescue Remedy; Mother was in Utah, and Dad and Luke were in the yard draining gasoline from cars before sending them into the crusher. At one point, Luke, who was seventeen at the time, dropped a gasoline-filled bucket; oil flowed out and soaked his trousers. It was hot outside, so the oil dried up quickly and they forgot all about it. As Luke readied a cutting torch, the spark ignited his leg.

Unable to get out of his gasoline-soaked jeans and howling like an animal, Luke somehow reached the house. Unsure what to do, Tara, who was only ten, tried different options before taking a dirty garbage bin, covering it up on the inside with a plastic bag, filling it up with ice-cold water, and asking Luke to dip his leg into it. Richard and, sometime later, Dad, turned up. After moving him into the shade, they waited for Mother. On returning, she applied her own salve on the burns and gave Luke an oil blend for the pain, while Tara wished they had some morphine. Dad asked everyone to lie about the incident as they didn't want the government to find out. Eventually, in about a month, Luke could stand up and move about.

Even eighteen years later, while writing the memoir, Tara remained unsure of where Dad had been as Luke arrived at the house alone. She remembered noticing some burns on Dad's hands so he might have stayed back to put out the brushfire. He probably set Luke in his truck's driver's seat, put it in first gear and, putting his faith in the dictum "The Lord will provide," let him roll alone to the house delirious.

CHAPTER 8: TINY HARLOTS

Eager to get away from the junkyard, Tara took up babysitting and cashew packaging jobs in the village at age eleven. Instead of money, she began taking piano lessons from one of her employers, Myrna, finally ending up in the dance classes offered by Myrna's sister, Caroline.

For a Christmas dance recital, the girls had to wear sheer tights, which made Tara think of them as tiny harlots. After watching the recital, Dad was furious with Caroline for making young girls dress up like whores, and Mother sided with him, despite having known about the dress.

Feeling guilty about forbidding the dance classes, Mother managed to persuade a voice teacher to teach Tara. After a few lessons, the teacher got her to sing in front of the congregation at Sunday church. Initially nervous, she performed flawlessly. To her surprise, Dad seemed proud of her. He even offered to put up the money she would need if she got the lead in the staging of *Annie* in the town theater.

CHAPTER 9: PERFECT IN HIS GENERATIONS

Tara's performance in *Annie* was in the summer of 1999. Interacting with other "normal" children was awkward for her, but she found confidence through her perfect dialog delivery. She also met Charles, a friendly boy her age, at the rehearsals.

Dad was in the front row when the play opened. He bought tickets for the next night as well and never stopped Tara from joining other plays, despite his reservations regarding the "kind of cavorting" taking place in the theater.

That winter, Tara would often suffer from a sore throat because of her tonsils. As a remedy, Dad suggested standing in the sun with her mouth open, which she followed dutifully, without much relief.

The other topic that kept him occupied around the time was Y2K. Convinced that the civilized world would come to an end on December 31st, he made the family spend all their money on supplies and a fifty-caliber rifle to keep the looting masses away. The modern-day Noah's excitement turned to abject disappointment as midnight came and went and everything kept functioning normally. God had withheld the flood.

CHAPTER 10: SHIELD OF FEATHERS

The Y2K disappointment brought on another low period for Dad that January. The family decided to make another trip to Arizona. Grandma-over-in-town had cancer and was taking a lot of medicines. This annoyed Dad, and he abruptly decided to drive the family back to Idaho one evening.

Richard drove for a while; then Dad took over and began speeding on the ice-covered road. In the resulting accident, Tara hurt her neck badly. Mother called an energy specialist, but the neck remained immobile.

Then, Shawn turned up after having stayed away for six years. He had a reputation for violence and wasn't familiar with Tara. About two months after the accident, Tara was working in the kitchen when Shawn walked up behind her and jerked her head with a swift, savage motion. After the initial shock, she began noticing a gradual improvement in her condition. The violent, compassionate act made her see in Shawn the father she wished Dad were, "some longed-for defender, some fanciful champion, one who wouldn't fling me into a storm, and who, if I was hurt, would make me whole" (Kindle Locations 1656-1658).

CHAPTER 11: INSTINCT

This was followed by another incident where Shawn came to Tara's rescue. She had been gifted a gelding by a great-uncle, and Shawn helped break him. Shawn had taken up horses in a serious way because he wanted to stay away from trouble in the town.

One summer evening, fifteen-year-old Tara was on the gelding, now called Bud, and Shawn was riding a new mare. While riding up the mountain, the mare kicked Bud in the chest, who went berserk and took off with Tara on her back. Shawn somehow managed to get the unbroken mare to move into place beside Bud, took the horse's reins, and got him to stop before Tara could get hurt.

CHAPTER 12: FISH EYES

Tony had taken out a loan to buy his own rig and had to keep the truck on the road to make the payments. When his wife got sick, Tony asked Shawn to run the rig for a week or two. Shawn agreed but wanted Tara to come along. Tara spent the next few days traveling with Shawn between Albuquerque and Washington State, playing word games, having fun on the CB, and learning martial arts at truck stops.

Sometime later, Shawn drove Tara to an audition for a new play and met seventeen-year-old Sadie there. Over the next few days, Tara was confused by Shawn's rude and unpredictable behavior with Sadie, who clearly adored Shawn. He also said Sadie had "fish eyes" behind her back— "They're beautiful, but their heads're as empty as a tire" (Kindle Locations 1807-1808).

One night, he came home after spending time with Sadie and asked Tara for some water. She fetched it but jokingly dumped it over his head. In a flash, he grabbed her hair, pulled her into the bathroom, and dropped her head into the toilet. Thinking it was over, as she began moving away, he seized her wrist and kept twisting it until she apologized. After he'd left, Tara hated herself for her weakness, the fact that anyone could hurt her like that. She forced herself to believe that this did not affect her, only to realize much later that it not affecting her was its effect.

CHAPTER 13: SILENCE IN THE CHURCHES

The twin towers fell that September; Tara, fifteen, had never heard of them till then. There were short-lived fears of further attacks or army drafts, which helped Tara forgive Shawn. Audrey got married to Benjamin, a local farm boy three days later at the age of nineteen.

The physical changes that come with adolescence both thrilled and frightened Tara. During this time of confusion, comments from Dad about other women's hemlines and necklines left a deep mark on her. "I would remember the words very often in the years that followed, and the more I considered them, the more I worried that I might be growing into the wrong sort of woman" (Kindle Locations 1905-1906).

Shawn saw Tara talk to Charles at the auditions and began commenting on her makeup, people thinking she was "that kind of girl," and her being just like the rest. He also started calling her "fish eyes" and a whore. Things came to a head when Shawn confronted Tara violently in front of Mother and insisted she was a whore even though she pretended to be "saintly and churchish." Tara was saved from worse physical torture because Tyler turned up unannounced and Shawn wasn't willing to confront his brother.

Later, Shawn, as usual, came back to apologize, making Tara feel that maybe she was the one in the wrong. She felt he knew more about worldly women and made him promise he'll keep her from becoming one.

Tyler's presence embarrassed Tara more than her treatment by Shawn. But talking to Tyler was also the first time she thought of going to Brigham Young University (BYU) in Utah, which accepted homeschoolers.

CHAPTER 14: MY FEET NO LONGER TOUCH EARTH

College had been irrelevant to Tara till then. She had assumed she would get married by nineteen, her husband would build a house on some corner of Dad's farm, and she would become the next midwife. Encouraged by Tyler, she began studying for the ACT. She managed to teach herself most of the math, but required tutoring from Tyler to understand trigonometry.

Shawn had been working as Dad's foreman on a job to build industrial granaries in a nearby town. Tara was at Aunt Debbie's home one evening when Mother called her to tell her about Shawn's accident at the building site.

The reports were conflicting. It seemed that Shawn had fallen twelve feet from the roof and hit his head hard. He was disoriented, and Dad just asked him to take a break. About fifteen minutes later, he began getting violent. Luke and Benjamin tried to hold him down when he hit his head all over again and lay still. Someone finally called 911.

On regaining consciousness, Shawn insisted on seeing Tara, but she took her own time to get there. Feeling guilty for her initial delay in reaching him, she quit her job and began tending to him as he recovered gradually. Being at home also gave her time to prepare for the ACT.

The accident made Shawn even more unpredictable and violent. Tara would clean the toilet every morning out of the fear that her head might be inside before lunch. Thinking about it later, she wasn't sure if his personality had changed all that much, but she had convinced herself then that it had.

CHAPTER 15: NO MORE A CHILD

That winter, as she was sitting with her parents, there was a moment of epiphany for Tara (now sixteen) when she realized that there was no future that could hold both her father and her as a woman with independent thought. "I would remain a child, in perpetuity, always, or I would lose him" (Kindle Locations 2205-2206).

Dad had clearly stated he was against her trying to get into BYU, but she was surprised Mother wanted her to "burst out of here in a blaze." Tara needed a twenty-seven at least on the ACT to have a chance at admission, but her first attempt didn't go too well.

To make matters worse, Dad started charging her for small things when he realized she was hoarding her paychecks for tuition. He even threatened to throw her out as she was old enough to pay rent now. She was more hurt when Mother asked if she could move out. However, the greatest shock came when Tara realized Mother didn't even know how old she was. Mother was convinced Tara was at least twenty and agreed to let her stay only after realizing that she was just sixteen.

CHAPTER 16: DISLOYAL MAN, DISOBEDIENT HEAVEN

One evening, Tara was studying at Grandma-over-in-town's place to retake the ACT, when Shawn turned up to watch a movie with her. Shawn was confident she'd get her twenty-seven and get to college. He left for home before her on his motorcycle. Driving back in a happy stupor, she came upon Shawn lying in a pool of blood by the side of the road.

Dad asked her on the phone to take Shawn back home for Mother to treat her using her potions, but she chose to take him to the hospital.

She knew opting to go to the hospital was major defiance of Dad's rules. He never brought it up again, but she knew they had come across a fork on the road, and she had gone one way and he the other.

The ACT results came out three weeks later. She got a twenty-eight and applied to BYU a week later. Soon after, she received the admission letter. Mother was ecstatic and helped her find an apartment in Utah, but Dad began picking up fights for small reasons. By Christmas that year, as she waited for the term to start on January 5, she was certain that "something terrible was coming, something that would obliterate everything I'd known before" (Kindle Locations 2491-2492).

PART II

CHAPTER 17: TO KEEP IT HOLY

Tara's early days at college were filled with instances of cultural shock—Mormons behaving like gentiles and working on the Sabbath—and revelation of how little her "education" had taught her. Having been late in registering for freshman-level courses, she managed to squeeze into introductory courses in English, American history, music, and religion and a junior-level course on art in Western civilization.

While the "essay form" of writing or names like Cicero and Hume were new to her, the most embarrassing instance was when she casually asked her Western art professor what the Holocaust was. The professor and the entire class assumed she had picked this topic to fool around, which didn't help her conviction that everyone thought of her as a freak. She had heard of the Holocaust once in her childhood but had always thought of the number of casualties being about half a dozen, not in millions.

CHAPTER 18: BLOOD AND FEATHERS

Tara found it difficult to get along with her roommates, partly because of her different standards of hygiene. To her mind, if the stench of rotting fruit in the fridge or dirty dishes in the sink was bearable, the house was clean. She also never used soap except when she showered, usually once or twice a week, and sometimes not even then.

Apart from an impending financial crisis, she was also worried by Western Civ. Waiting for the results of an exam in the course, she wrote in her journal: "I don't understand why I wasn't allowed to get a decent education as a child" (Kindle Locations 2668-2669). Being in college reminded her of the injured owl Luke had found when she was very young. After recovering a little in their care, it grew restless. They had to let it go before it healed fully because Dad told them it had a better chance of survival in the wild. It didn't belong and couldn't be taught to.

She failed the exam, and desperate to tell someone of this failure, called home. Dad picked up and, to her surprise, asked her not to worry about the money. This tenderness helped her, but she knew that it wouldn't last and the endless struggle between them would return.

She managed a B in the next exam, thanks to having figured that she needed to read the textbook and not just look at the pictures, and was pulling As by the end of the semester.

CHAPTER 19: IN THE BEGINNING

Back home during the semester break, Tara was forced to work in the junkyard by Dad. She started dating Charles. She would work the whole day, wash away all the dirt carefully in the evening, and put on some makeup before meeting Charles outside the house.

She passed all her courses, earning As in all except Western Civ., which qualified her for scholarship for half the tuition.

There was a moment of tenderness with Charles a few weeks later, but the continuous remembrance of the word "whore" kept her from getting too close to him.

CHAPTER 20: RECITALS OF THE FATHERS

Dad and Shawn became comrades in making Tara's life difficult because they felt she had become uppity. Shawn called her names like "wench" and "Wilbur (the pig)," especially in front of Charles. Once, her face was covered with grease after a hot day in the junkyard, and Shawn began calling her "Our Nigger."

He had called her this earlier, too, but it had never held much significance for her. At college, she got to know of the African American struggle for the first time. Now, every time she was called the word, her mind went to the dehumanization and brutality that her people had played a role in.

CHAPTER 21: SKULLCAP

The day before she returned to BYU, Tara was suffering from a bad earache. On Charles's insistence, she took a painkiller and was surprised by the almost-immediate relief. She had always relied on her mother's (ineffective) lobelia and skullcap tincture for all pain.

Back at college, she had new roommates, including a very sympathetic senior called Robin. Tara failed the midterms, was finding algebra difficult, almost stopped sleeping, developed ulcers, and took up a difficult janitorial job to make money. Afraid to ask for help, she managed to speak to her algebra professor on Robin's advice. He told her anyone who could get a perfect score on the final would get an A, irrespective of the midterm score.

CHAPTER 22: WHAT WE WHISPERED AND WHAT WE SCREAMED

Tara was home for Thanksgiving. A dinner with Charles present turned ugly when Shawn assaulted her again. She was mortified that Charles had seen her like this. Over the next few days, she began venting her resentment for Dad and Shawn on Charles, and they eventually broke up. He told her that he loved her, but only she could save herself.

Back at college, the ulcers returned, and an injury to one of her toes kept getting worse. She refused to see a counselor but managed to get an A in algebra.

During Christmas break, she learned Richard was preparing for the ACT as well. Pressure from Dad, who was convinced Richard was a genius, was making him nervous, though.

One evening after work, Tara was at a town store with Shawn. She hadn't had the time to wash up. Charles was entering the store, and not wanting him to see her all messy, she refused to go in. Shawn could smell her embarrassment and dragged her out. The scene soon turned horrifying, with her clothes almost coming off. Forced to go in, she kept laughing so that everyone would think this had been a friendly spat. Back home, she wrote it had felt like being beaten by a zombie. Shawn returned later with ice wrapped in a towel and told her the next time they were having fun, she should tell him if something is wrong.

CHAPTER 23: I'M FROM IDAHO

Tara was approached by men at the Mormon Church, but she discouraged them. The bishop, a friendly man whom she went to several times later to discuss her problems, spoke to her about the importance of marriage. She knew about it and even wanted it, but getting close to a man scared her. Dad and, later, Shawn had often used the word "whore" in relation to her, which made her feel there was something impure in the fact of her being.

Shawn came to her help a couple of times when she faced money issues until the bishop convinced her to apply for a government grant. She had to sneak into her home like an intruder to get a copy of her parents' tax returns for the grant, which strengthened her belief that she was not a part of Buck's Peak any longer.

CHAPTER 24: A KNIGHT, ERRANT

Having sufficient money in her bank account for the first time allowed Tara the luxury to focus on her courses. She learned about bipolar disorder in Psychology 101 and wrote an accusative paper on the effect bipolar parents have on their children. She also learned the truth behind the Ruby Ridge incident—the Randy Weaver story Dad had told them about years earlier.

She decided to experiment with normality. She started going out with Nick but was afraid to talk about her family with him.

One day, out of the blue, she got a frantic call from Audrey. Dad had been in an accident, and Tara needed to come home urgently.

CHAPTER 25: THE WORK OF SULPHUR

Dad had been in a fuel tank explosion in his junkyard, which had completely melted the lower half of his face and his fingers. The family almost lost him, but layers upon layers of Mother's Rescue Remedy salve (and diligent care from everyone) eventually saved him.

Tara visited Buck's Peak for a while, but she didn't want Dad to get infected by her own strep infection, so she went back to the campus. She continued to feel uneasy sharing all of this with Nick.

CHAPTER 26: WAITING FOR MOVING WATER

For Tara, the apprehension about Dad's ability to cope with being dependent on others was mixed with the hope for some change in him; for once, he was forced to be a listener rather than the speaker.

Shawn and Emily, a girl he had met sometime earlier, announced their engagement around this time. Tara tried to convince her she shouldn't marry someone she was afraid of, but she could see that Shawn had the same hold on Emily that he had had on Sadie. Tara's inability to say anything at their wedding in September left her anxious.

Her growing distance with Nick had been apparent for some time, and she broke up with him a week after the wedding.

CHAPTER 27: IF I WERE A WOMAN

Tara had gone to college primarily to study music, but she found herself being drawn to courses on geography, history, and politics. Wondering if there was something wrong in being a woman and drifting towards such subjects, she approached her Jewish history professor, Dr. Kerry. As Dr. Kerry learned more about her background, he advised her to stretch herself and apply to a study abroad program at Cambridge. She applied and, despite an initial rejection, managed to get through.

Christmas break at Buck's Peak was like being in a different world, as usual. Dad attributed his recovery to the Lord's mercy and Mother's Miracle Salve. The entire episode had grown to take the form of a myth in the local community. Emily had a difficult pregnancy around this time; that the prematurely born baby managed to survive was taken as another sign of the Lord's gifts to the family.

CHAPTER 28: PYGMALION

Tara was intimidated by the stately King's College at Cambridge; this feeling of not belonging didn't really leave her through her stay there. So the praise from her research supervisor, Professor Jonathan Steinberg, for her essay came as a shock. "I could tolerate any form of cruelty better than kindness" (Kindle Locations 3850-3851).

Professor Steinberg also assured her that he would make sure she got accepted into whatever institution she chose for graduate school. She was still not convinced she belonged, but words of encouragement from Dr. Kerry their last night at Cambridge helped.

"You are not fool's gold, shining only under a particular light. Whomever you become, whatever you make yourself into, that is who you always were. It was always in you. Not in Cambridge. In you. You are gold. And returning to BYU, or even to that mountain you came from, will not change who you are. It may change how others see you, it may even change how you see yourself—even gold appears dull in some lighting—but that is the illusion. And it always was" (Kindle Locations 3886-3891).

CHAPTER 29: GRADUATION

Tara applied for a Gates Cambridge Scholarship and, thanks to the strong recommendation from Professor Steinberg, got it. This turned her into a minor celebrity on campus and in Idaho.

Dad was miffed, though, as she hadn't mentioned homeschooling in any of her interviews. He and Mother didn't turn up at the functions she received awards at. They did come to the airport to drop her off because Dad seemed hopeful till the last moment Tara would stay back.

PART III

CHAPTER 30: HAND OF THE ALMIGHTY

At Trinity College, Tara dived wholeheartedly into picking up knowledge that was new to her and regular stuff for everyone else. Bob Marley's words "Emancipate yourselves from mental slavery" affected her deeply, as did the idea that "feminism" was more than just a word of ridicule. The most comforting learning, however, was John Stuart Mill's line: "Of the nature of women, nothing final can be known." This brought relief to years of uneasiness, of feeling that there was something unnatural about her yearning.

At Buck's Peak, during Christmas break, she found that Mother's Miracle Salve had begun selling well. Richard had married Kami, a "mainstream" Mormon, had a one-month-old son, and was finishing his undergraduate degree in chemistry at Idaho State.

One night, when everyone was home, the door burst open and Emily rushed in bawling. Shawn, because of some minor issue, had exploded with anger and thrown her out of their trailer into the snow. This was nothing new for the family, but Tara and, more importantly, Kami, were there to see this. Tara would wonder later if she should have spoken out at this point.

CHAPTER 31: TRAGEDY THEN FARCE

Just before returning to England, Tara visited Audrey and her young daughters. An inconsequential comment made her realize, much to her shock, that Audrey had suffered Shawn's violence as well.

A proper response from Audrey came through email sometime later, where she appeared to believe Tara and planned to confront Shawn and their parents. Tara's instinct was to ask Audrey to wait, but Audrey spoke to Mother anyway. Within a few hours, Mother and Tara were discussing this online. Mother seemed suitably repentant and agreed that she should have protected Tara.

A phone conversation a week later gave the impression that the issue was being dealt with. Mother had grown a successful business; Dad had softened after the accident, and Tara was convinced they would force Shawn to get help.

In the meantime, Tara became more comfortable with life at Cambridge. She enjoyed a group trip to Rome, submitted a well-received paper, and finally seemed to let go of the shame she'd felt about her family.

CHAPTER 32: A BRAWLING WOMAN IN A WIDE HOUSE

Back at Buck's Peak in autumn, Tara was surprised to see how huge Mother's oils business had grown. Grandma-down-the-hill, who had suffered from bone marrow cancer for nine years, passed away, and Dad went into depression again for a while. On being left on his own to manage breakfast one morning, Dad asked Tara to prepare it as she was a woman, reminding her once again of the distance that had sprung up between the two of them.

CHAPTER 33: SORCERY OF PHYSICS

Audrey wanted Tara to stay longer as it was difficult to confront their parents alone. Tara returned, feeling guilty but realizing that Cambridge felt more like home. "Sometimes I felt damned for those feelings. No natural sister should love a stranger more than a brother, I thought, and what sort of daughter prefers a teacher to her own father?" Tara also finally had a boyfriend, Drew, in whom she could confide everything about her family.

At Christmas, she had been back at Buck's Peak only for a short while when Shawn asked her along on a car drive. During their talk, he threatened to kill Audrey if she didn't shut up with her accusations.

CHAPTER 34: THE SUBSTANCE OF THINGS

Tara decided to mention this to Dad right away. To her surprise, Dad began accusing her of conspiring to send Shawn to prison. No support came from Mother.

Tara shut herself in the bathroom, looking at her weeping face in the mirror. She was very aware that this was the same place where Shawn had forced her face into the toilet and made her confess that she was a whore.

Having regained a fragile sense of calm, she wanted to go to bed, but Dad had asked Shawn to come over. Tara was scared now. Shawn came in agitated, sat down beside her, and placed a small knife glowing crimson with fresh blood in her palm. Dad began a long lecture on how girls need to be taught how to behave; at the end, Shawn said a perfunctory sorry and hugged her.

Tara escaped early next morning. She got to know later that the blood had been from Shawn's dog, Diego. Diego had apparently been killing Luke's chickens and needed to be put down, but Tara was sure it had been pure rage. It also occurred to Tara later that Mother had lied about things being dealt with.

CHAPTER 35: WEST OF THE SUN

In March, Tara received an email from Shawn with a chapter from the Bible and a single verse set in bold: *O generation of vipers, how can ye, being evil, speak good things?* This was followed by a call where he threatened to kill her. Tara's parents still refused to believe her. A series of such calls followed, only stopping when Shawn ended all relations with her. Dad called her hysterical, and both he and Mother felt she deserved this treatment.

Sometime later, Audrey informed Tara by email that Dad had visited her; she had atoned for her sins, and would like

Tara to keep away from her. Tara knew she had lost her entire family then because Dad was sure to do the same with everyone.

CHAPTER 36: FOUR LONG ARMS, WHIRLING

Tara was at Harvard on a fellowship; Mother messaged that she and Dad were coming to visit. Tara realized this was their last attempt to "save" her. During the trip, there were the usual lectures from Dad. Tara knew that surrendering would be a relief, but she couldn't make herself do it. Calling her a sinner, Dad and Mother left abruptly.

CHAPTER 37: GAMBLING FOR REDEMPTION

Tara had gone through periods of intense self-doubt since the conflict with her family began. Following her parents' visit, she also started having episodes of sleep-walking. She first lost interest in all extra-curricular activities; then, she stopped studying. All her time was spent on catching up on TV series.

Against Drew's advice, she flew back to Idaho in the hope of repairing the damage. The visit, however, made her realize once again that life with Dad was like a puzzle whose rules she would never understand. This was the last time she would talk to him. Tara did get a call from Tyler, who seemed to believe her.

In the next few weeks, as she moved back to England from Harvard, she would suffer a panic attack, send an unanswered mail filled with accusations to Dad, and wonder if her studying and thinking had turned her into someone who didn't belong anywhere.

CHAPTER 38: FAMILY

Tara was failing her PhD but couldn't explain the reasons to her sympathetic supervisor.

Tyler called her to tell her he had confronted Dad, but had been threatened with disownment. Tara was sure she was about to lose the one sibling she was close to.

A few days later, she received mail from Tyler and his wife, Stefanie, which, unexpectedly, expressed full support for her and criticized their parents for their resistance to change. This inspired her to enroll with the university counseling service. She gradually recovered over several sessions and began focusing on her thesis—an evaluation of Mormonism's place in the larger human story.

Soon after her 27th birthday, nearly ten years after she first set foot in BYU, she successfully defended her dissertation to earn her PhD.

CHAPTER 39: WATCHING THE BUFFALO

Back in Idaho, Tara first visited Grandma-over-in-town. She was suffering from Alzheimer's and couldn't recognize Tara, but the short talk with Grandpa was cordial enough. She messaged Mother, who refused to meet unless Tara agreed to meet Dad. "Mother's message amounted to an ultimatum: I could see her *and* my father, or I would never see her again. She has never recanted" (Kindle Locations 5054-5055).

Tara did decide to take a look at the house at Buck's Peak before leaving. She had heard Mother's business was booming, and the renovated house reflected that. She had also heard of Dad mistreating employees, including Mom's sister, Angie.

Tara visited Aunt Angie and, when Grandma-over-in-town died, met up with other relatives on Mother's side, who seemed more willing to accept her. At the funeral, all the siblings turned up. She realized everyone, except Tyler and Richard, was dependent economically on Dad and Mother and, thus, unlikely to rebel.

Tara would return to Idaho in a year, but would only meet Angie and Grandpa as Mother continued with her stance.

CHAPTER 40: EDUCATED

In the present time, Westover hasn't seen her parents for years. She gets news from Buck's Peak through Richard, Tyler, and Tony.

Peace didn't come easily. She spent two years actively enumerating Dad's flaws, hoping the justification would lessen her guilt. Realizing that guilt is the fear of one's own wretchedness, she eventually learned to accept her decision on its own terms.

With the distance between her and Dad, she can better appreciate his tender qualities that had got lost in his towering indignation at close quarters. She can love him better this way.

"But what has come between me and my father is more than time or distance. It is a change in the self. I am not the child my father raised, but he is the father who raised her.

...No matter how much I appeared to have changed—how illustrious my education, how altered my appearance—I was still her. At best I was two people, a fractured mind. She was inside, and emerged whenever I crossed the threshold of my father's house.

...You could call this selfhood many things. Transformation. Metamorphosis. Falsity. Betrayal.

I call it an education" (Kindle Locations 5141–5153)

KEY THEMES

THE TRANSFORMATIVE POWER OF EDUCATION

It was through education that Westover was able to get out of the life of marriage, child-bearing, working on the farm, and being dependent on a man that she had long believed she was heading toward. Her education didn't just open her up to the many experiences her life in Idaho had kept her from, it also encouraged her to think for herself and recognize (and raise her voice against) the damaging aspects of life on her parents' farm.

THE DEEP HOLD OF PATRIARCHY

The overbearing roles played by Westover's father and her brother Shawn are recurring themes in the memoir. Her father's almost tyrannical rule over the family forced his wife to work as a midwife against her wishes, kept their children from school or proper health care, left emotional scars on the children's psyche, and, eventually, created a deep schism. Shawn, keeping up the tradition of brooking no opposition, physically and emotionally abused his sisters, comfortable in the belief that the family would side with him.

THE CONSTANT PRESENCE OF RELIGION

Even though some of her parents' beliefs, like faith in muscle testing, did not conform to the Mormon doctrine, religion did play a dominating role in the daily lives of the Westover family. It was the driving force behind the decisions to eschew education and modern medicine, Dad's strong belief in the End of Days, strict rules regarding clothing, or shunning of their daughter for her imagined sins.

THE EXISTENCE OF TWO AMERICAS

While this is not as explicit a theme as the other three, the distance traveled by Westover from rural Idaho to Harvard brings into stark contrast the great divide between "mainstream" America and the communities that continue to be distrustful of much that modern America stands for.

EDITORIAL REVIEW

"Haunting" and "unforgettable" are words so often used by publishers eager to get their books selling that when a book does come along that merits these adjectives, using the words feels almost like a disservice. Tara Westover's *Educated* will haunt you though, even if you have read your fair share from the genre that sneering critics have dubbed "misery lit."

Tara Westover's survivalist father held views that were conservative even by the general standards of his Mormon community, and the family often bore the brunt of these quaint opinions. Her mother comes across as slightly more pragmatic but, true to the expectations from a woman in this milieu, believed in supporting her husband. As a result, Westover, the youngest of seven children, could never go to school; the family wasn't allowed to access formal health care; talking to a man outside the family or dressing inappropriately got you labeled a "whore;" and raising one's voice against an abusive male family member got cruelly dismissed as hysteria.

Despite having lived an isolated life for the first seventeen years of her life, Westover taught herself science and math, went on to receive a PhD from Cambridge, and studied at Harvard on a fellowship. In the process, she was disowned by her parents and went through an extended period of crisis of faith (in education). As the memoir ends, one can see that the dust hasn't yet settled on this story. The wounds are still raw, and hope remains in her that issues will eventually get resolved.

There has been much conversation in recent times regarding sections of the US that do not seem to be connected to the mainstream. Much like J.D. Vance's *Hillbilly Elegy*, this book adds meaningfully to this conversation, with insights that are interesting, if not as explicit.

Even though Westover has hinted on a number of occasions that this is her version of the events, it is hard not to feel anger and horror while going through them. The many near-fatal accidents involving the family, followed by the carelessness with which the injured are treated, make one wonder how Westover survived relatively unharmed. And, while there may not be any notable physical scars, her emotional and psychological scarring is obvious.

In fact, her life has been so littered with traumatic events and so overshadowed by an overbearing father and brother that it becomes difficult to catch a glimpse of the real young woman through all of it. That Westover is an extremely intelligent, determined, thoughtful, and hard-working person is never in doubt, but her personality fails to appear more than the sum of the effects of her family members' deeds.

But, apart from being a minor blemish in this otherwise eminently well-written first book, this is probably a deliberately created effect. Because if *Educated* demonstrates the immense power of education to transform lives, it also shows how the sins of parents leave excruciatingly deep marks on their children.

BACKGROUND ON AUTHOR

Tara Westover is a historian by profession. She was born in Idaho in September 1986 to Mormon survivalist parents, who did not support formal education, modern medicine, or the government. Like many of her six elder siblings, she never went to school but managed to teach herself enough to gain admission to Utah's Brigham Young University. After a difficult first year, she graduated *magna cum laude* in 2008. Supported by a Gates Cambridge Scholarship, she earned her MPhil from Trinity College in 2009. She was a visiting fellow at Harvard University in 2010. After her return to Cambridge, she completed her PhD in 2014.

Educated, the internationally best-selling memoir, is her first book and relates her childhood and youth in a small Idaho farming town, her relationships with her parents and siblings, and her transformation through education. The book, released in 2018, became an immediate *New York Times* bestseller and received glowing reviews from *The Atlantic Monthly*, *USA Today*, and *The Economist*, among others. It has been voted one of NY Times' 10 Best Books of 2018, won the top spot in the Memoir and Autobiography category in the Goodreads Choice Awards and been included in President Obama's annual summer reading list.

END OF BOOK SUMMARY

Made in the USA
Middletown, DE
20 June 2019